The message at the heart of Christianity is really quite simple—simple enough to be outlined in a few pages. It is a message from the Bible about God and his son, Jesus. It is about life and death, and the choice that we all face.

And it all starts with a loving creator God...

1 God is the loving ruler of the world.

He made the world.

He made us rulers of the world under him.

You are worthy, our Lord and God, to receive glory and honour and power, for you created all things, and by your will they were created and have their being.

Revelation chapter 4, verse 11

But is that the way it is now?

t he first point of the Christian message is that God is in charge of the world. He is the ruler, the supreme president, the king. Unlike human rulers, however, God always does what is best for his subjects. He is the kind of king you'd like to be ruled by.

God rules the world because he made the world. Like a potter with his clay, God fashioned the world into just the shape he wished, with all its amazing details. He made it, and he owns it.

He also made us. God created people who were something like himself, and put them in charge of the world—to rule it, to care for it, to be responsible for it, and to enjoy all its beauty and goodness. He appointed humanity to supervise and look after the world, but always under his own authority, honouring him and obeying his directions.

You can see this represented in the illustration above: God is the ruler (the crown) and humanity is created to live in and rule God's world under God's loving authority.

It all sounds rather ideal—God in heaven, people ruling the world according to his directions, and everything right with the world. But everything is very obviously not right—with us or the world.

2 We all reject the ruler—God—by trying to run life our own way without him.

But we fail to rule ourselves or society or the world.

There is no-one righteous, not even one; there is no-one who understands, no-one who seeks God. All have turned away.
Romans chapter 3, verses 10-12

What will God do about this rebellion?

t he sad truth is that, from the very beginning, men and women everywhere have rejected God by doing things their own way. We all do this. We don't like someone telling us what to do or how to live—least of all God—and so we rebel against him in lots of different ways. We ignore him and just get on with our own lives; or we disobey his instructions for living in his world; or we shake our puny fists in his face and tell him to get lost.

How ever we do it, we are all rebels, because we don't live God's way. We prefer to follow our own desires, and to run things our own way, without God. This rebellious, self-sufficient attitude is what the Bible calls 'sin'.

The trouble is, in rejecting God we make a mess not only of our own lives, but of our society and the world. The whole world is full of people bent on doing what suits **them**, and not following God's ways. We all act like little gods, with our own crowns, competing with one another. The result is misery. The suffering and injustice that we see around us all go back to our basic rebellion against God.

By rebelling against God, we've made a terrible mess of things. The question is: what will God do about it?

3 God won't let us rebel forever.

God's punishment for rebellion is death and judgement.

Man is destined to die once, and after that to face judgement.

Hebrews chapter 9, verse 27

God's justice sounds hard. But...

G od cares enough about humanity to take our rebellion seriously. He calls us to account for our actions, because it matters to him that we treat him, and other people, so poorly. In other words, he won't let the rebellion go on forever.

The sentence God passes against us is entirely just, because he gives us exactly what we ask for. In rebelling against God, we are saying to him, "Go away. I don't want you telling me what to do. Leave me alone." And this is precisely what God does. His judgement on rebels is to withdraw from them, to cut them off from himself—permanently. But since God is the source of life and all good things, being cut off from him means death and hell. God's judgement against rebels is an everlasting, God-less death.

This is a terrible thing, to fall under the sentence of God's judgement. It is a prospect we all face, since we are all guilty of rebelling against God.

Is that it then? Are we all destined for death and everlasting ruin? If not for God's own miraculous intervention, we would be.

4 Because of his love, God sent his Son into the world: the man Jesus Christ.

Jesus always lived under God's rule.

Yet by dying in our place he took our punishment and brought forgiveness.

Christ died for sins once for all, the righteous for the unrighteous, to bring you to God.
1 Peter chapter 3, verse 18

But that's not all...

because of his great love and generosity, God did not leave us to suffer the consequences of our foolish rebellion. He did something to save us. He sent his own divine son into our world to become a man—Jesus of Nazareth.

Unlike us, Jesus didn't rebel against God. He always lived under God's rule. He always did what God said, and so did not deserve death or punishment. Yet Jesus did die. Although he had the power of God to heal the sick, walk on water and even raise the dead, Jesus allowed himself to be executed on a cross. Why?

The Bible rings with the incredible news that Jesus died as a substitute for rebels like us. The debt that we owed God, Jesus paid by dying in our place. He took the full force of God's justice on himself, so that forgiveness and pardon might be available to us.

All this is quite undeserved by us. It is a generous gift, from start to finish.

But that's not all...

5

God raised Jesus to life again as the ruler of the world.

Jesus has conquered death, now gives new life, and will return to judge.

In his great mercy he has given us new birth into a living hope through the resurrection of Jesus Christ from the dead.

1 Peter chapter 1, verse 3

Well, where does that leave us?

G od accepted Jesus' death as payment in full for our sins, and raised him from the dead. The risen Jesus is now what humanity was always meant to be: God's ruler of the world.

As God's ruler, Jesus has also been appointed God's judge of the world. The Bible promises that one day, he will return to call all of us to account for our actions.

In the meantime, Jesus offers us new life, both now and eternally. Now, our sins can be forgiven through Jesus' death, and we can make a fresh start with God, no longer as rebels but as friends. In this new life, God himself comes to live within us by his Spirit. We can experience the joy of a new relationship with God.

What's more, when we are pardoned through Jesus' death, we can be quite sure that when Jesus does return to judge, we will be acceptable to him. The risen Jesus will give us eternal life, not because we have earned it, but because he has died in our place.

Well, where does all that leave us? It leaves us with a choice of only two ways to live.

6 | The two ways to live

A. Our way:
- Reject the ruler—God
- Try to run life our own way

Result:
- Condemned by God
- Facing death and judgement

B. God's new way:
- Submit to Jesus as our ruler
- Rely on Jesus' death and resurrection

Result:
- Forgiven by God
- Given eternal life

Whoever believes in the Son has eternal life, but whoever rejects the Son will not see life, for God's wrath remains on him.

John chapter 3, verse 36

Which of these represents the way you want to live?

We can continue in our rebellion against God, and try to run our lives our own way without him. Sadly, this is the option that many people persist in.

The end result is that God gives us what we ask for and deserve. He condemns us for our rejection of his rightful rule over our lives. We not only have to put up with the messy consequences of rejecting God here and now, but we face the dreadful prospect of an eternity of separation from him, without life or love or relationship.

For those of us who have realized that our situation is hopeless, there is a lifeline. If we turn back to God and appeal for mercy, trusting in Jesus' death and resurrection, then everything changes.

For a start, God wipes our slate clean. He accepts Jesus' death as payment for our sins, and freely and completely forgives us. He pours his own Spirit into our hearts and grants us a new life that stretches past death and into forever. We are no longer rebels, but part of God's own family as his adopted sons and daughters. We now live with Jesus as our ruler.

The two ways to live could not be more different, and they present you, the reader, with some choices.

The first question you must ask yourself is: Which way do I want to live?

If your answer to the question above is 'my own way', then you probably don't believe some or all of the message we have been outlining. Perhaps you do not believe that God is going to judge rebels, or that you really are a rebel. If that is the case, then please think carefully. It would be a good idea to investigate thoroughly the claims that have been made here, because if they are true, the consequences are life and death.

Perhaps you could get hold of a modern translation of the Bible and read about it for yourself (Mark's Gospel is a good place to start). Or you could talk to a Christian friend, or contact the publisher of this booklet for more information.

However, if you know that you are a rebel against God, and would prefer to live his way, the next obvious question is: **What can you do about it?**

1. Talk to God

The first thing to do is to talk to God. You need to admit before him that you have rebelled against him, that you deserve punishment, and that you're asking for mercy on the basis of Jesus' death in your place. You'll also need to ask God to help you change from being a rebel to being someone who lives with Jesus as their ruler. You could pray something like this:

Dear God,

I know that I am not worthy to be accepted by you. I don't deserve your gift of eternal life. I am guilty of rebelling against you and ignoring you. I need forgiveness.

Thank you for sending your son to die for me that I may be forgiven. Thank you that he rose from the dead to give me new life.

Please forgive me and change me, that I may live with Jesus as my ruler. Amen.

The first step, then, is to pray.

2. Submit to Jesus

The second step is also fairly obvious. Having prayed the sort of prayer above, you will want to start putting it into practice—that is, actually submitting to Jesus. There will no doubt be all kinds of areas in your life in need of change. You'll need to get rid of old rebellious habits (like greed, anger, selfishness, and so on) and start some new ones that please God (like generosity, kindness, love and patience).

This second step will go on for the rest of your life, but God will be with you all the way. He'll keep speaking to you (through your reading of the Bible); he'll keep listening to you and helping you (as you pray to him); he'll empower you to change and to live his way (by his Spirit who lives within you); and he'll provide brothers and sisters to encourage you along the way (as you meet with other Christians).

The second step, then, is to submit to Jesus and start living with him as your ruler.

3. Keep trusting

The third thing you have to do is also ongoing. You need to keep putting your trust in the right place. It's only because of Jesus (and his death and resurrection) that you can be forgiven and put right with God. You'll need to keep coming back to this again and again, because as you start to live God's new way, you will still fail and do the wrong thing. We all do. We all need to keep looking back to the death of Jesus on the cross as the only grounds for our pardon. We must never stop relying on him—and him alone—as the means by which we are forgiven and granted eternal life.

If you know full well that you have not yet taken these steps, and that you are still an unforgiven rebel, then you need to do something about it. You are at a fork in the road. It's the choice that we all face. There are only two ways to live.